CONTENTS

Introduction to Parents and Caregivers

☼ Your 7-year-old wonders if there is poison in her food.
She can't eat a meal without asking, and often can't eat the meal at all.

☼ Your 12-year-old has to do everything in multiples of two,
growing frantic if he loses track or is interrupted.

☼ Your 9-year-old apologizes incessantly, fearful she might have
offended someone.

Obsessive-compulsive disorder is about more than hand washing. It's about thoughts and urges that get stuck in your child's mind, terrifying him, tormenting her. It's about rituals intended to ward off harm. It's about things feeling "not right" to your child. And it's about questions, endless questions—questions about safety, questions about certainty, questions that drive you crazy, questions that break your heart.

OCD is a neurobiological problem, and there is nothing you or your child did to cause it. While it appears random and bizarre, it's actually quite common and predictable. OCD is related to certain abnormalities in brain chemistry and function. And although it appears rather tenacious, it is in fact a treatable condition.

Children with OCD benefit most from a type of therapy called cognitive-behavioral therapy. Cognitive-behavioral therapy teaches children new ways to think about and respond to the thoughts and urges that characterize OCD. Children learn, in effect, to retrain their brains to respond more accurately and efficiently – to become unstuck.

What to Do When Your Brain Gets Stuck teaches children and their parents the cognitive-behavioral techniques used to conquer OCD. In language that is both humorous and reassuring, this book presents a new framework for understanding OCD, as well as a set of skills to bring it under control. Practice of these skills is essential if your child is to move from understanding to actual mastery. Throughout this process, you will be your child's coach, empowering him to learn effective tactics, cheering her budding success.

This book will be most effective when read by a parent and child together. Give ample time to absorb new ideas by reading slowly, just one or two chapters at a time, and by encouraging your child to draw and write as directed. Between reading sessions, talk to your child about the concepts in this book, referring back to the stories and metaphors. Use the language your child is learning. Gentle humor helps many children shift perspective when they are stuck, so do use humor, especially as it is modeled in these pages. At the same time, remember that fighting OCD might well be the most

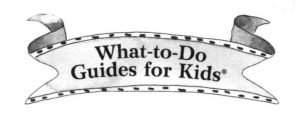

What-to-Do
Guides for Kids®

What to Do When Your
BRAIN
GETS STUCK

A Kid's
Guide to
Overcoming
OCD

by Dawn Huebner, Ph.D.

illustrated by Bonnie Matthews

MAGINAT   TON, D.C.

To Wiley Rasbury, Ph.D., whose knowledge base and calm presence have benefited so many children, and a legion of young psychologists. I am honored to have worked with you. And to Tamar Chansky, Ph.D., whose books *Freeing Your Child from Anxiety* and *Freeing Your Child from OCD* are must-reads for parents and therapists alike. I greatly admire your work. – DH

What to Do When Your Brain Gets Stuck is part of the Magination Press What-to-Do Guides for Kids® series, a registered trademark of the American Psychological Association.

Published by
M A G I N A T I O N   P R E S S
An Educational Publishing Foundation Book
American Psychological Association
750 First Street, NE
Washington, DC 20002

For more information about our books, including a complete catalog, please write to us, call 1-800-374-2721, or visit our website at www.maginationpress.com.

Library of Congress Cataloging-in-Publication Data

Huebner, Dawn.
What to do when your brain gets stuck : a kid's guide to overcoming OCD /
by Dawn Huebner ; illustrated by Bonnie Matthews.
p. cm. – (What-to-do guides for kids)
Summary: "Teaches school-age children cognitive-behavioral techniques to reduce thoughts and images related to obsessive-compulsive disorder, through writing and drawing activities and self-help exercises and strategies. Includes introduction for parents"—Provided by publisher.
ISBN-13: 978-1-59147-805-8
ISBN-10: 1-59147-805-7
1. Obsessive-compulsive disorder in children—Juvenile literature.
I. Matthews, Bonnie, ill. II. Title. III. Series.
RJ506.O25H84 2007
618.92'85227—dc22   2006034529

Manufactured in the United States of America
10 9 8 7 6

difficult thing your child has ever done. Be generous with your encouragement and support.

Please read this entire book before presenting it to your child. OCD is as bewildering to parents as it is to kids. You will be a more effective coach if you have an understanding of the techniques presented here and of the principles underlying them.

Children master OCD through *exposure* and *response prevention*. While these terms are not used in the text of the book, they are the guiding principles behind each of the tools presented. The idea is to teach children to experience an OCD thought or urge without trying to neutralize it with a ritual. Checking, asking, repeating, and redoing are all rituals. The two steps of (1) not doing the ritual and (2) learning to manage the accompanying nervousness until it recedes desensitize children, reducing their responsiveness to OCD. *What to Do When Your Brain Gets Stuck* walks your child through this process, breaking down exposure and response prevention into manageable steps, rendering OCD powerless.

What to Do When Your Brain Gets Stuck can be used alone or as a companion to therapy. If your child is already in therapy, please talk to the therapist about this book. If your child is not in therapy but has intrusive thoughts and repetitive behaviors like those described in this book, please speak with your child's medical doctor to determine the possible need for therapy.

As you are learning about OCD, think about *The Wizard of Oz*. Take yourself back to the first time you saw the movie. Do you remember how powerful, how utterly terrifying the wizard seemed? The wizard was an invisible force, ruling an entire land through his threats and commands. Everyone jumped to follow his orders. The alternative was simply too frightening to consider. But as you know, the Wizard of Oz was a sham.

You and your child are going to learn that OCD is like that wizard holding your child hostage in some foreign land. Of course, it isn't enough to simply tell your child that OCD's threats are empty. Your child is going to have to experience it for him- or herself. *What to Do When Your Brain Gets Stuck* will help your child do just that. It will give your child the power to come home again.

CHAPTER ONE

Are You Saving Junk?

Close your eyes for a moment, and picture your house. Take an imaginary walk through each of the rooms, counting all the garbage pails you see. Think of the kitchen, the bathrooms, the bedrooms, every single room. How many garbage pails are there all together? Write your number here.

We all throw stuff away every day.

Take a peek in the garbage pail closest to you. You don't have to touch anything. Just look inside.

☼ Draw three things that are in the garbage pail closest to you.

☼ Now think of two other things that you've thrown away recently. Add those to the pail.

☼ Ask whoever is reading this book with you to tell you something they have thrown away today. Draw that in, too.

Usually we don't think much about garbage. We don't have classes in "garbage-ology," and we don't read books on the subject (except this one!). We just know what needs to be thrown away, and we toss it. That's because we have something that works like a sorting machine in our brains.

This sorter is able to tell the difference between important stuff and junk. It's not something we really have to think about. Our brains automatically tell us "garbage!" and we throw that thing away.

Once in a while, we might not know for sure whether to keep something, so we ask, or we keep it for a little while to see if we end up needing it. But usually it isn't an issue. We know what's worth keeping, and we keep it. We know what's garbage, and we throw it away.

☼ Circle the things that are worth keeping.

☼ Put an X over the things that should be thrown away.

☼ Put a question mark over the things you aren't sure about.

9

But what if we didn't know any of that? What if the brain sorter that tells us what to keep and what to throw away wasn't working right? What if we thought that *everything* was equally important, that *everything* should be saved?

Here's what that would look like. You would have about 7,000 empty toilet paper rolls. Your toy box would be full of plastic cases and twist ties and all of the things that surround toys when you buy them. Empty cereal boxes would be stacked in your cabinets, and empty milk cartons would be crammed into the refrigerator. You would have a drawer full of T-shirts you've outgrown and broken shoelaces and nail clippings. And those branch-like stems from grapes. And dried-up glue sticks. You would have piles of broken toys and used tissues. And you would save it all.

If you didn't have a brain sorter, your whole house would be a giant mess. Your closets would be overflowing. And if you wanted to use the flashlight you got for your last birthday, you would have to move aside about a hundred empty packages to reach it, and then you would need to try 20 batteries before finding a couple that still worked.

It would be pretty frustrating, wouldn't it? And you would wind up wasting lots and lots of time. But that's exactly what would happen if you didn't know how to sort the important stuff from the junk.

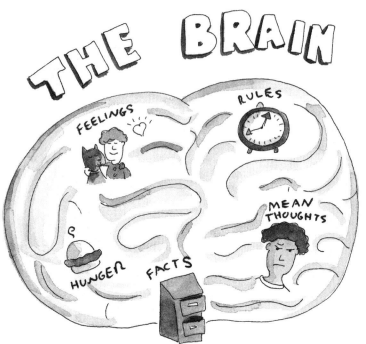

Fortunately, we do have brain sorters to keep our houses from getting so cluttered. We also have brain sorters to keep our *brains* from getting cluttered.

Brain sorters check each thought that comes into our heads and decide where that thought needs to go.

If we think about taking a bite or a drink, our brain tells our arm to reach for the burger or the glass. If we learn something new about lizards, our brain puts that information into its Reptile Facts file. If we think about pinching someone who's bothering us, our brain sends that mean thought right into the brain garbage, because that thought is a piece of brain junk.

So, just like all of the good stuff and garbage that exists in the real world, our thoughts need to be sorted out too. Some thoughts are worth keeping. Some need to be thrown away.

☼ Circle the thoughts that are interesting, important, or fun. Those thoughts are worth keeping.

☼ Put an X through the thoughts that are best to put in your brain garbage pail.

Sometimes it's easy to know which thoughts to keep and which thoughts to throw away. But sometimes it isn't so easy. Sometimes junk thoughts take a little piece of something true and exaggerate it, making it seem real. Sometimes they tell you something bad is about to happen, when really you are safe. And sometimes brain sorters simply get mixed up.

When this happens, junk thoughts end up in the **SAVE** pile. They say you need to do things a certain way to be safe. They make you feel unsure. Before you know it, they have taken over your life.

14

If this has happened to you, if it's hard for you to feel safe or sure of yourself because of your thoughts, it might be that your brain sorter has a glitch. A glitch is when things aren't working quite the way they should. Your brain sorter has gotten stuck, so even your junk thoughts are getting tossed into the SAVE pile, and your brain isn't sending out the "oh, that's garbage" signal, like it used to.

You aren't crazy and you aren't doomed. You just have something called OCD. And the good news is that there are things you can do to get your brain sorter working again. But first you need to know a bit more about OCD.

What Is OCD?

OCD stands for obsessive-compulsive disorder.

Obsessions are thoughts that go through your head over and over again. You don't want to be thinking these thoughts, but they are there anyway, making you feel nervous or bad.

Compulsions are the things you do to get rid of the bad thoughts and nervous feelings. They are actions you take over and over again, not because you want to, but because it seems like you have to. Compulsions often become rituals, which means they have to be done the same way every time.

Here's how OCD works. First you have a thought, like "What if I have some germs on my hand?" Then you have a fear, like "If I have germs on my hand, I'm going to get sick. If I get sick, I'll throw up." You certainly don't want to throw up, so you decide to do something. You decide to wash your hands to take care of the germs that might be on your hands that might make you throw up.
So you wash your hands, and then you feel better.

It doesn't seem like such a big deal. Washing your hands takes only a minute. But it doesn't stop there, because OCD ALWAYS WANTS MORE.

To understand this better, let's talk about grocery shopping. You've probably seen something like this…

A mom and her child have just finished shopping. They are both hungry and maybe a little cranky because there is a long line to check out. Finally it's their turn, and the mom starts to unload the food from the cart. Suddenly the child spots the candy, rows and rows of it, right next to the cart. It looks so good!

☼ Draw your favorite kind of candy in the empty space on the shelf.

The mom says no. She already has lots of food, and it's almost lunch time. But the child wants the candy. He really, really wants it. It's right there, and it would taste so good, and he can't believe his mom said no. So he starts to cry. The mom keeps unloading the food. Now the child really wails. He tells his mom she is mean and says he is going to starve to death if he doesn't get a candy bar. He has a tantrum, right there in the store.

The mom is tired, and she's embarrassed by the child's tantrum. She just wants it to end. So she gives in. The moment she says OK and hands the child a candy bar, the tantrum stops. The child happily eats the candy.

What's going to happen the next time this mom and her child go to the store?

If you said the child will demand candy again, you're right. The child will ask for candy, and he'll have a tantrum if his mom says no. He knows that if he makes enough of a fuss, his mom will give in. The child has learned that having a tantrum is a good way to get what he wants.

OCD is like that spoiled child.

It's not that OCD sits in a shopping cart, kicking and screaming for candy. In fact, you can't see OCD at all. But you can imagine OCD as a little pest inside your head, demanding things and causing lots of trouble.

OCD is determined to get its way. Just like the child who tells his mom he's going to starve to death if he doesn't get the candy, OCD tells you that bad things are going to happen if you don't do what it wants. This is pretty scary, so most kids feel like they have to listen. Or else!

Draw that pesky OCD having a tantrum.
What bad things does OCD say
will happen if you don't listen?

Think back to that scene in the grocery store. Let's imagine it a different way.

What if, no matter how loud and ugly the tantrum got, the child's mom told him no? What if she showed him she wasn't going to listen by paying for the groceries and leaving the store without buying any candy?

The mom might be kind of embarrassed, but she would get over it. And the child wouldn't *really* starve to death. Actually, nothing bad would happen at all.

In fact, something pretty good would happen.

The next time the mom said no, the child would have a rip-roaring tantrum to see if he could get her to change her mind, like she used to.

But if his mom didn't give in, the child's next tantrum wouldn't last for quite so long.

And the next time, and the next time, and the time after that, the child would learn that when his mom says no, she means it.

There's no point to having a tantrum if the tantrum doesn't get you what you want.

So the child would stop having tantrums.

Now think about OCD again. You've been giving in to OCD, because it's been frightening you, making you feel miserable inside. But each time you give in, each time you do what OCD wants, you're handing OCD the biggest, most delicious candy bar in the world. You're showing OCD that bothering you is a good way to get what it wants. So OCD demands more. And more. And more.

You're probably tired of OCD's tantrums. You probably want them to end.

This book is going to teach you to stop OCD's tantrums. It's going to teach you the tricks that OCD plays to frighten you. And then you're going to learn some tricks of your own, but we're going to call them tools. These tools will put you back in charge.

CHAPTER THREE

OCD's Favorite Tricks

Have you ever seen a magic show? Magicians do amazing things, such as making coins disappear and changing the color of scarves. Magicians know lots of tricks to make it seem like these things are happening. But as you know, most tricks are just optical illusions.

Optical illusions are things that trick your eyes. They make your brain think it is seeing something that isn't really true.

Here's one you can try. Later you can trick your friends with it:

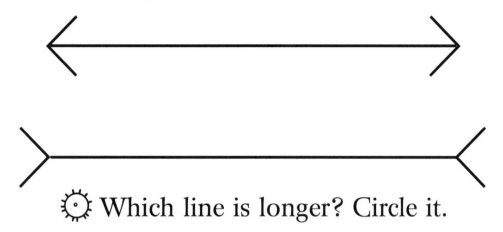

☼ Which line is longer? Circle it.

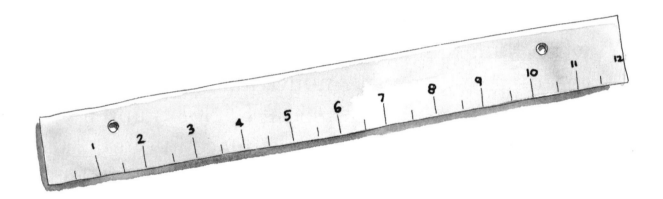

☼ Get a ruler and measure the two lines.

They are exactly the same length, aren't they? The arrows on the ends of the lines tricked your brain into thinking that the lines were different. Even though the bottom one looks longer and the top one looks shorter, they're really both the same.

Some tricks are fun, and some tricks aren't. OCD plays tricks on your brain that aren't fun because they frighten you. But once you know the tricks, they aren't quite as scary. See if you can begin to recognize when OCD is playing these tricks on you.

OCD'S FIRST TRICK: SOUND THE ALARM

Our brains are set up to respond quickly when things might hurt us. When we see a car speeding toward us or notice a snake slithering in the grass, our brains shout DANGER! and a series of changes quickly take place in our bodies. These changes give us a burst of energy, making us alert and getting our muscles ready to run away or fight or do whatever is needed to keep ourselves safe. This is called the fight-or-flight response, and it happens automatically whenever the brain alarm gets triggered.

OCD tricks kids by sounding false alarms. It's like OCD is pulling a fire alarm in your brain. Your body springs into action, because that's what bodies do. But even though the alarm is clanging like crazy, even though your body is ready to fight or run away, there isn't really a fire. It's a false alarm. OCD is trying to trick you.

What dangers does OCD try to trick you about?

POOF!

OCD'S SECOND TRICK: THE MAYBE GAME

Most of the time, kids make decisions based on what is most likely. It's hard to be totally sure, and you don't need to be totally sure anyway.

Could there be a sparrow in your bathroom? Not likely, but *maybe*.

When you go into the bathroom to brush your teeth, you don't check for sparrows first. You don't open the shower curtain looking for sparrows before you step into the bathtub. In fact, you probably aren't thinking about sparrows at all.

But OCD likes to trick kids, to frighten them and waste their time by making them worry about things they wouldn't normally be thinking about.

So OCD says,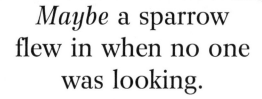

> *Maybe* a sparrow
> flew in when no one
> was looking.
>
> *Maybe* there's sparrow-doo on the bathroom floor.
>
> Sparrow-doo is dirty.
>
> *Maybe* you'll step in it.

Yuck! Who wants to step in sparrow-doo?

Then OCD makes something up, and tells you that you need to do that thing to keep yourself safe.

> You need to check
> the *whole* bathroom
> every time you go in.

So whenever your dad tells you to go brush your teeth, whenever you need to use the toilet or get in the tub, you check for sparrows first. You carefully open the medicine cabinet, and you look in the bathtub. You check the bathroom window to make sure it isn't open. You have to do the whole check in a certain order to make sure you don't leave any parts out. So you chant quietly in your head while you do it, to keep yourself on track,

Behind the door? *Nope.*

In the cabinet? *Nope.*

Shower? *Nope.*

Towel closet? *Nope.*

It takes a lot of time, but you need to be sure. Your dad gets annoyed and asks what's taking so long. Then you have to check again because you lost your place. You keep thinking about that sparrow-doo. Did you really check everywhere? *Maybe* the sparrow flew in while you were looking behind the door. You'd better check again.

That's OCD's Maybe Game. You think about what might happen, even though it isn't very likely, and you have to do something to protect yourself, just in case.

Think about how OCD plays the Maybe Game with you.

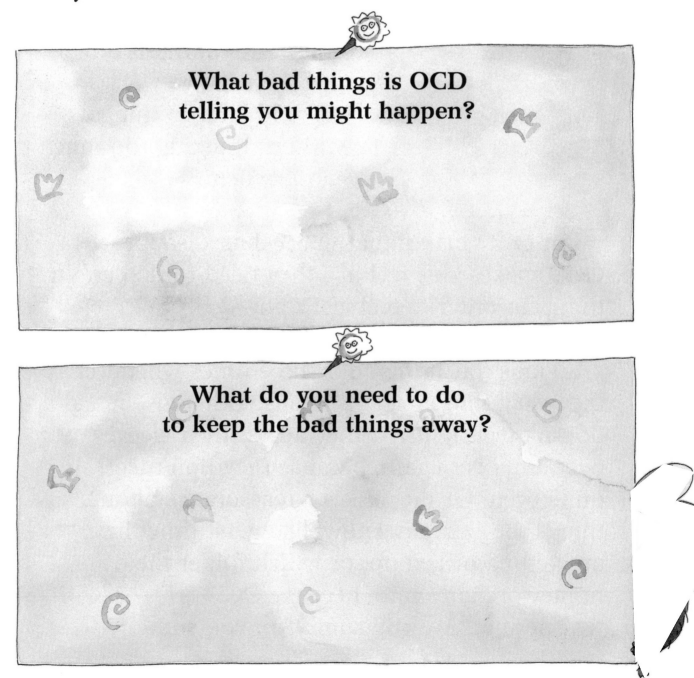

What bad things is OCD telling you might happen?

What do you need to do to keep the bad things away?

OCD'S THIRD TRICK: THE DISAPPEARING JUST-RIGHT FEELING

Most of the time, we feel OK. We don't notice the way our hair feels on our head or our socks feel on our feet. We don't notice what it feels like to enter a room or sit down on a chair. We walk around and do things without thinking too much about them.

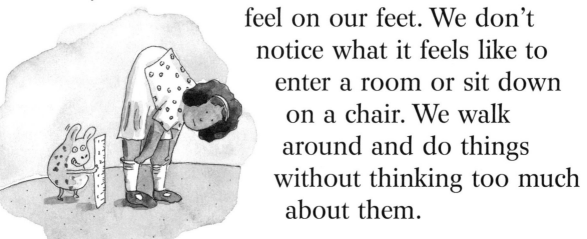

But OCD makes that OK feeling disappear. OCD makes kids feel like they need to do certain things in order to feel just right again.

So kids touch the door three times whenever they walk into a room, because otherwise it doesn't feel right. Or they adjust their sleeves over and over again, because they don't feel quite even. Or they ask for reassurance about things they already know, like what time they are getting picked up, or which folder their homework goes into, because OCD is whispering, "Are you sure? Are you sure?"

When kids do these things, they aren't thinking that something bad is going to happen. They just know they don't feel quite right. So they do these things to get that just-right feeling back again. But really, it's an OCD trick.

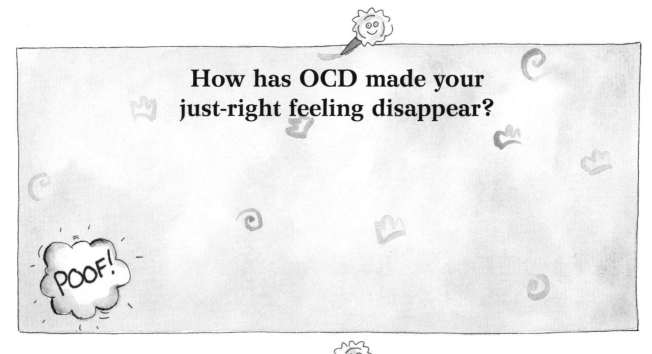

How has OCD made your just-right feeling disappear?

POOF!

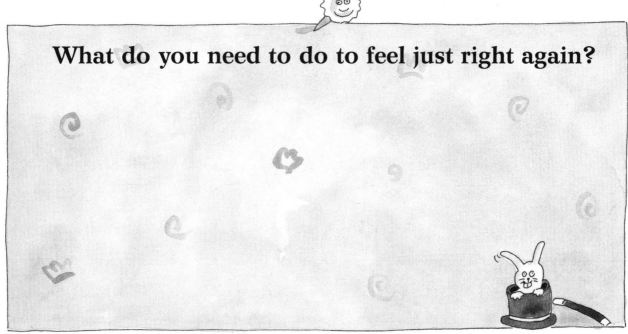

What do you need to do to feel just right again?

That's it. That's OCD's entire act, just those three tricks:

SOUND THE ALARM

THE MAYBE GAME

THE DISAPPEARING JUST-RIGHT FEELING

Your brain has been falling for those tricks because they seem so real. Like the optical illusion at the beginning of this chapter, OCD's tricks are very convincing. But once you know more about OCD and begin using the tools described in this book, OCD's tricks will stop working on you.

You are about to stop being fooled.

Why Do Kids Get OCD?

We are talking about OCD like it's a pest who throws tantrums, or a strange magician whose tricks frighten you.

But really, OCD is only a mechanical blip in your brain. Your brain is like a big computer, and OCD happens when a tiny part of that computer gets programmed wrong, so it stops doing what it's supposed to do. That's it.

You might be thinking, "What?"

You might be thinking, "No way!"

But it's absolutely true. OCD is a system error in your brain, no more dangerous than a hiccup.

Having OCD does not mean that you're brain damaged. In fact, there are lots of very smart people with OCD. OCD just means that the way your brain sorts and delivers messages doesn't always work the way it should.

There are two main message problems.

We have already talked about the first one, when things get sorted incorrectly in your brain. Thoughts that belong in the junk pile go into the important pile and get stuck there.

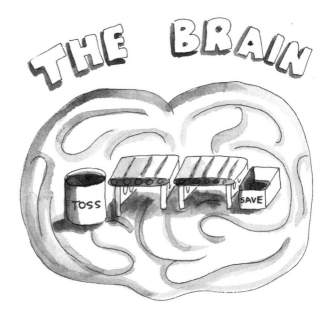

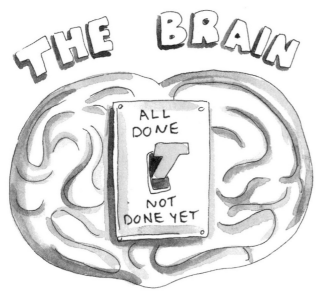

The other message problem has to do with the "all-done" switch in your brain. The all-done switch tells your brain when something is finished.

☼ Draw some clothing in this dryer.

Have you ever noticed the way a clothes dryer works? Wet clothes get put in, and the dryer sends out heat while it tumbles the clothes around. When the clothes are dry, the dryer shuts off.

But how does the dryer know when the clothes are dry?

Dryers have a little sensor that tells them when the clothes are dry. When the sensor senses dryness, the dryer automatically shuts off.

Your brain has a sensor too. Your brain's sensor lets you know when an action is done. When you close a door, your brain tells you, "OK, it's closed now." When you erase a mistake on your homework, your brain says, "You got it, time to move on." This message system is important, because if you don't get the all-done signal from your brain, you don't know when to stop.

OCD plays around with this message system. It stops your brain from letting you know that you're done. So kids with OCD feel like they need to do things again and again.

They need to give the door an extra push to make sure it's closed, because their brain doesn't tell them it's closed the first time.

They need to re-read words, to make sure they saw them all.

They need go to the bathroom again and again.

They need to spend hours on their homework and say goodbye three times and redo all sorts of things because their brains aren't sending out the "OK, you're done" message.

What are some things you feel the need to re-do?

So, why do these brain problems happen? Why does the sorting system put thoughts in the wrong pile? Why does the delivery system fail to give the all-done signal?

Some brains are more sensitive to these problems than others. It's something you are born with. It's not because you're bad, or because your brain somehow got broken. It's the way some brains are set up.

You might be surprised to find out that there are over one *million* kids in the United States who have OCD, and more in the rest of the world. And there are lots and lots of kids who are learning about their OCD and learning what to do about it, just like you.

And the really interesting thing is that you can do something about it. You can actually teach your brain to sort things into the right piles. You can learn to give yourself the all-done signal. You can be like a repair-person, using tools to make some adjustments, helping your brain to work more smoothly again.

OCD FIGHTING TOOLS

Is the Job Too Big?

It might seem like it's going to be a lot of work to get rid of OCD. It might seem like it's going to be *hard*.

Kids with OCD often aren't sure they want to do anything about it, because fighting OCD seems awfully scary. Many kids wonder if the job is too big for them.

☼ Draw yourself standing at the bottom of this staircase.

If someone told you to go all the way to the top without touching any of the stairs in between, you would say, "I can't." That would be much too hard.

But if someone told you to take one step, you could do that. And then you could take one more. And one more. And eventually you would be at the top. The way to get to the top of a staircase, even a really tall staircase, is to climb one step at a time.

You already know that. In fact, you've probably climbed lots of staircases in your life.

You've probably taken on tough challenges, too. You've learned to do things you weren't sure you would ever be able to do, like ride a bike without training wheels or sculpt animals out of clay.

Think about something that once was really hard but now you know how to do.

Draw or write about it here.

☼ What steps did you take to learn how to do this?

☼ Was just one step enough?

☼ How did you keep yourself going,
    even when it was tough?

   Take a minute to talk to your mom or dad about
a hard thing you learned to do.

   We are going to get rid of OCD one step at a time.
You can make each step as big or as small as you want.
You get to decide. And it doesn't really matter whether
you take a whole bunch of small steps or a few big
steps, because either way you will get to the top.

One More Thing You Need to Know

Remember the fight-or-flight response? It's a series of changes that automatically happen in your body when your brain's alarm system gets triggered. Even during false alarms, remember? Your whole body revs up for action, and you feel super-charged.

Sometimes this super-charged feeling feels good, like when you go flying down a hill on a sled or when you reach into a basket of squirming, nipping, squealing puppies to pick out the one that's going to be yours. In these cases, you probably feel excited rather than scared.

WOOF!
WOOF!

Think of something you love to do that makes you feel super-charged, something a little risky that gives you a thrill.

Draw or write about it here.

Whether the changes that happen in your body during the fight-or-flight response feel good or bad depends on the thoughts inside your head. If you're busy thinking about getting hurt or being in danger, the extra charge in your body is going to make you feel terrified. If you're thinking, "Wheeeeeeeee! This is fun!" you're going to feel excited instead.

Think about roller coasters.

Some kids love roller coasters. Their hearts beat wildly while they ride. These kids feel thrilled as they charge up and down the hills. They come out laughing at the end.

Other kids hate roller coasters. Their hearts beat wildly, making them think they are going to go flying over the edge. They dread each hill and grip the bar tightly, desperate for the ride to end. These kids come out looking shaky and sick.

It's the very same roller coaster. In both cases, the fight-or-flight response has gotten triggered and kids' hearts are pumping fast. But whether that feels like a good thing or a scary thing depends on the thoughts in each child's head.

Now think about OCD. OCD trips the alarm in your brain. Your body springs into action with the fight-or-flight response. And then comes the most important part: your thoughts.

OCD is screaming DANGER!, so kids with OCD begin thinking about being in danger. They feel like they need to *do* something to keep themselves safe and get the bad feelings to go away.

But you know what? The fight-or-flight response fizzles out on its own. Nervous feelings flare up and fade, faster than you might imagine, as long as you don't feed them with scared thoughts. So those uncomfortable feelings end, and nothing bad happens, even if you don't do what OCD wants you to do.

To understand this, let's talk about going to the movies.

☼ Draw yourself walking into this theater.

☼ Fill in the sign with the name of your favorite movie.

Here are three questions for you to think about:

1 Pretend it's a summer day. It's so hot outside. When you first walk into the air-conditioned lobby it feels – brrrrrrr – cold! But after a little while, it doesn't seem so cold anymore. Why is that?

2 You walk into the theater where the movie is going to be shown, and it's dark! You can hardly see well enough to find an empty seat. But pretty soon it doesn't seem so dark anymore. Why is that?

3 You sit down and wait for the movie to begin. When the movie first comes on – wow! – is it loud! But after a while the volume seems fine. Why is that?

Actually, the answer to all three questions is exactly the same.

☼ Write the answer on this movie screen.

You get used to it, right?

But what if you didn't know that.

Let's take the part about the sound. What if, when the movie comes on, it seems so loud that you go running out of the theater? You wait a little while, and then you get curious, so you go back in. Yow! It's still really loud. So you go back out to the lobby again. Back and forth you go, and each time it's just as loud as before.

Of course! If you leave the theater each time you notice the sound is loud, you never give your ears a chance to adjust. And you never get to see the movie either.

It's like that with the scared feelings that go along with OCD. You're going to be feeling uncomfortable inside. You're going to want to do whatever OCD says to make your nervous feeling end.

But remember:

The nervous feeling will end anyway, even if you don't listen to OCD. You just have to let yourself get used to it.

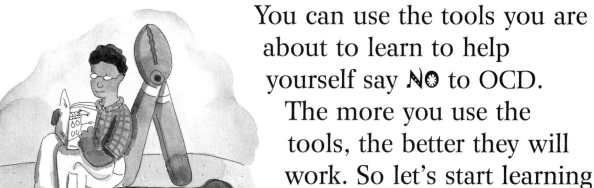

You can use the tools you are about to learn to help yourself say NO to OCD. The more you use the tools, the better they will work. So let's start learning the tools that will put you back in charge.

Your First Tool: I Spy

Your first tool is actually a game. It's called I Spy. You may have played it before. I Spy is when you look at a scene very carefully to find things that are hidden.

Look at this picture and see if you can find...

bug	**globe**	cupcake	pie
snake	**fork**	**baseball mitt**	shoe
hat	**tulip**	boat	purse
cake slice	**toothbrush**	**bell**	chest

Of course, OCD doesn't hang around in pet stores. OCD is in your brain, trying to hide amid your regular thoughts. You are going to learn to catch OCD.

To get good at this game, you need to be able to spot OCD with a sharp eye. Remember, OCD can have two parts: a thought (the O part) and an urge that follows the thought (the C part). An urge is a strong desire to do something, the feeling that you *must* do that thing.

Here are some OCD thoughts, and the urges that might follow them.

OCD THOUGHTS
My hands are dirty.
I might have cheated.
That lid isn't on tight.

OCD URGES
Wash.
Apologize.
Check to be sure.

Make a list of some of the OCD thoughts and urges that bother you.

OCD THOUGHTS

OCD URGES

59

Now you're starting to recognize what OCD looks like. Each time OCD pops into your brain with one of its thoughts, tell yourself, "That's OCD talking." Each time you get the urge to do an OCD thing, tell yourself, "OCD alert!"

You can get good at spotting OCD. You can tell yourself:

THAT'S JUST A BRAIN BLIP.

What can you say when you recognize OCD?

Your mom and dad can play I Spy with you.

Remember to practice, practice, practice. The more you play I Spy, the easier it will be to spot OCD each time it tries to hand you some junk. Soon you'll be able to tell the difference between the thoughts and urges you want to be having, and the thoughts and urges that OCD is causing.

Stay on this step as long as you need to. Look back at your list of thoughts and urges on page 59 to remind yourself what OCD sounds like and feels like. When you're ready, you can read on.

CHAPTER EIGHT

Your Second Tool: Talk Back

Kids are taught to be polite. Being polite is important because it shows respect for other people and it makes them like you more. When people are polite, the world is a better place for everyone.

Write three rules you know about being polite.

1

2

3

One rule about being polite is, "Don't talk back." Talking back means arguing. It means giving a sassy answer to something that was just said. Kids sometimes talk back to their parents when they don't want to do something their parents asked them to do.

It isn't OK to talk back to your parents. But it is OK to talk back to OCD.

It's OK to talk back to OCD, because OCD is a bully and bullies need to be stopped. So when OCD is trying to get you to listen, tell it **NO!**

Or picture OCD in place of the child at the grocery store, the one having a whopper of a tantrum.

Think of some ways to tell OCD to be quiet and leave you alone:

You don't have to listen to OCD. OCD is a brain blip. The things it says are tricks. So whenever OCD begins bothering you, talk back.

Your Third Tool: Show OCD Who's Boss

You have been spying OCD and talking back. That's two steps you've climbed. Draw yourself heading for the third step. You're doing great!

The next step is to show OCD who's the boss. (Hint: It's you!)

Remember the mom at the grocery store? She didn't stand there arguing with her son. She just said no and then got busy unloading the food.

You can do that, too. You can say no to OCD and then get busy with something else.

You have a bunch of choices about how to show OCD that you are the boss. Read about each of them before deciding which ones you're going to do.

HOW TO SHOW OCD WHO'S BOSS

Tell OCD, "I'm not going to do that right now." Make OCD wait 10 minutes. Get busy with something else that is interesting or fun. When you make OCD wait, it often gives up and goes away, so you don't feel the urge to do the OCD thing anymore.

CHOICE 1
DELAY

Tell OCD, "I'm not listening to you." Then leave the scene. If you're in your bedroom, for example,

and OCD wants you to change your socks because they don't feel right, leave your socks on and walk out of the room. Go to another part of the house and get busy with something else while your feet get used to the way your socks feel. Walking away reduces the power of OCD.

Tell OCD, "You're wasting my time." If OCD wants you to check your backpack three times, do it twice instead. After a few days, move from twice to once. If OCD makes you ask lots of questions, give OCD a question limit, like three questions a day. Don't let OCD go over the limit.

Tell OCD, "You're not my boss." If OCD wants you to wash your hands with your fingers first, then your palms, then the backs, change the routine. Do your wrists first, or skip your fingers, or rinse your hands without using soap. Do the ritual your way instead of OCD's way. Do it a different way every time.

This is a big step, but like all big steps, it gets you where you want to go the fastest. If OCD wants you to avoid doorknobs, grab a doorknob and hold it. Talk back to OCD. Say, "You're just trying to trick me. Stop fooling around with my brain." Then do something else, like make silly faces with your mom or read knock-knock jokes to your dad. Pretty soon your heart will stop pounding and that scared feeling will go away. Spend some time holding the doorknob every day, and soon it won't feel like a scary thing at all.

CHOICE 6 MAKE IT FUNNY

7, 2, 15

Tease OCD by turning what it says into something funny. If OCD wants you to do everything an even number of times, count in a crazy way to make OCD lose track of where you are.

If OCD is bugging you about throwing up, buy some plastic vomit and have a contest with your family to see who can do the funniest get-sick imitation. Really ham it up.

If OCD is making you think about a bad guy coming to get you, draw pictures of bad guys with watermelons cracked open on their heads and ants swarming up their legs.

Instead of trying to run away from the OCD thoughts that are bothering you, set aside time every day to think about them on purpose, but in a funny way.

You can do this even with the OCD thoughts that seem too terrible to tell. There are some pretty common OCD thoughts that make kids feel ashamed—thoughts about naked bodies and swear words and violent things. These are all examples of OCD just trying to freak you out. You aren't a bad kid for having these thoughts, and trying to push them out of your mind isn't going to work. So ask a grown-up to help you turn these thoughts into something ridiculous, or to help you think about them so often that your brain gets bored by them.

☼ Make a sign to help yourself remember your six choices.

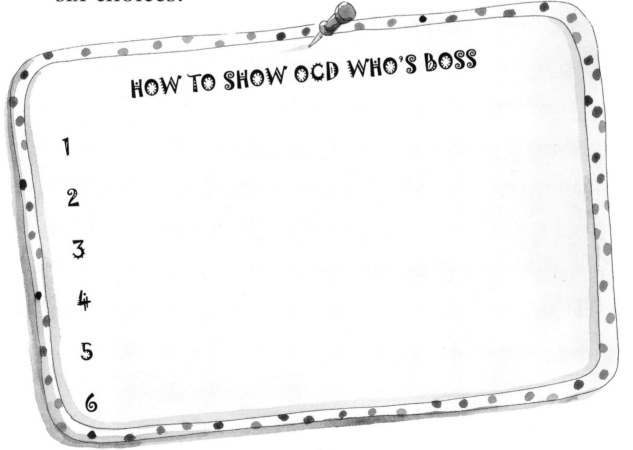

HOW TO SHOW OCD WHO'S BOSS

1

2

3

4

5

6

CHAPTER TEN

Putting Your Tools to Work

Now you know what you need to know to defeat OCD. It's time to put it all into action. Here's how it will work:

First, look at this measuring stick. You can use it to tell how uncomfortable or frightened you feel.

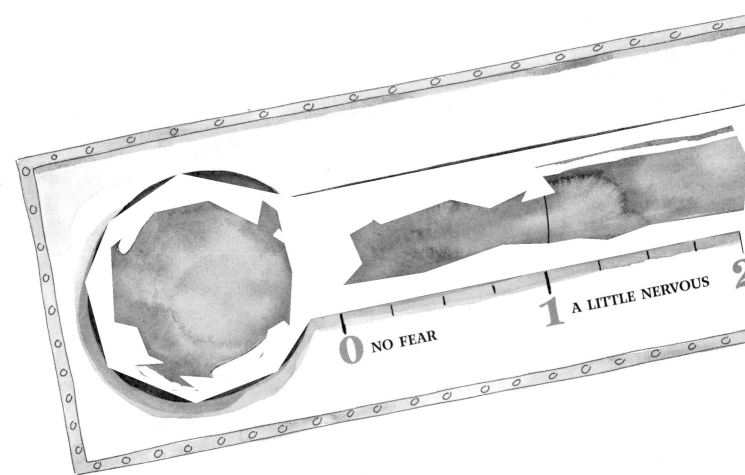

0 NO FEAR 1 A LITTLE NERVOUS 2

This fear measuring stick will also help you see how your fear trickles away over time, even when you don't do what OCD wants you to do. (Remember the movie theater?)

0 means you feel fine, not nervous at all. 5 means you are so scared you can't stand it, as scared as you've ever been in your life. Look at each of the numbers and what they mean.

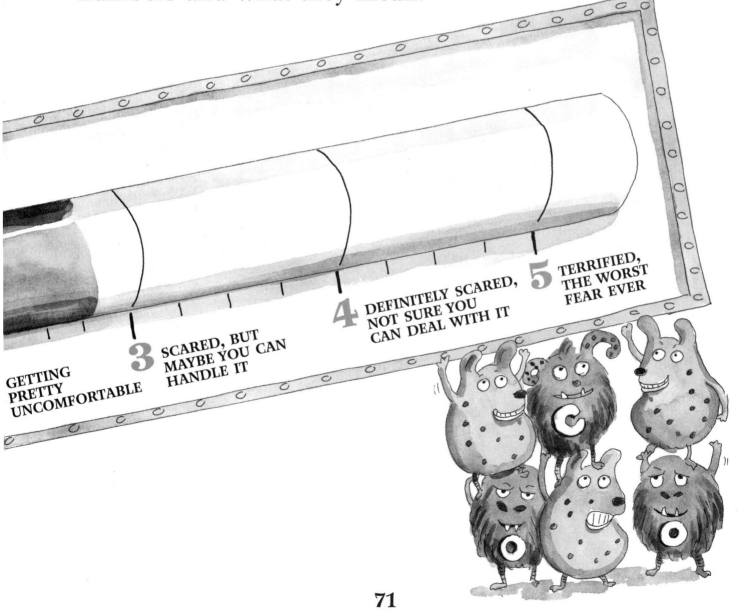

5 TERRIFIED, THE WORST FEAR EVER

4 DEFINITELY SCARED, NOT SURE YOU CAN DEAL WITH IT

3 SCARED, BUT MAYBE YOU CAN HANDLE IT

GETTING PRETTY UNCOMFORTABLE

Next, make a list of all the OCD thoughts and urges that bother you. Make your list as complete as you can. Leave the fear rating blank for now.

OK, now look at the list of OCD thoughts and urges that you just made. Going down the list, one item at a time, think about how scared you would feel if you said no to OCD about that thing. Use the fear measuring stick, and write your fear rating next to each OCD thought or urge.

Next comes the part you've been waiting for. You're going to take back control from OCD by picking the first way to resist.

As you're learning to say no to OCD, it's easiest to begin with urges. Remember that urges are compulsions, the C part of OCD. They are things like counting and checking and asking and washing, the things that you *do* to try to feel better. Look at your list on page 72, and find an OCD urge that you rated 3 or lower in the fear rating column.

If all of your OCD urges are rated higher than 3, see if you can break one down into smaller parts, so you can tackle one part at a time. For example, if OCD wants you to rewrite your homework until every letter looks perfect, say no to OCD on just your spelling papers. Don't worry about the rest of your papers for now.

What is the first OCD urge you're going
to say no to?

Write it here.

Next, pick one of the ways to show OCD
that you are the boss. Put a check mark next
to the method you're going to use.

☐ DELAY

☐ WALK AWAY

☐ GIVE OCD A LIMIT

☐ CHANGE THE RITUAL

☐ DO THE OPPOSITE

☐ MAKE IT FUNNY

Whenever the OCD urge you chose comes up, follow these steps:

1 Sound the OCD alert!

2 Talk back to OCD.

3 Use the method you chose to show OCD who's boss.

4 Right at the start of saying no to OCD, rate how you feel on the fear measuring stick.

5 Remind yourself that the scared feeling is just your fight-or-flight response.

6 Tell yourself that you are OK.

7 Tell yourself that you are not going to listen to OCD for at least 10 minutes.

OK! Now you're showing OCD who's boss. But your fight-or-flight response hasn't fizzled out yet. You're feeling a little (or a lot) scared. So what do you do?

Tell yourself you can do it.

Remind yourself it's an OCD false alarm, a major OCD tantrum, a brain hiccup.

Think about walking into a movie theater and getting used to the sound, or the dark, or the cold.

Then get busy doing something else. Have your dad test you on multiplication facts. Play with your dog. Eat your breakfast.

After 10 minutes, measure your fear again. If your fear is 2 or lower, you'll know that you're showing OCD it can't control you. Go for another 10 minutes, and watch your fear rating drop even lower.

When your rating gets to 1, you will know that OCD's tantrum is winding down. It will be easy to keep ignoring OCD now.

If your fear is 4 or higher, OCD is being stubborn with you. Don't give in. Try fighting OCD for another 10 minutes. If you're alone, get someone to help you. Two against one helps in the fight against OCD.

Each time your fear drops by at least 1 point, you will know that you're winning against OCD. You are teaching your brain to stop paying attention to OCD's messages. The more you fight OCD, the faster your brain will learn.

See if you can think of four things to do while you're showing OCD that you aren't going to listen.

Draw or write your ideas here.

NOT LISTENING TO YOU

OCD Is a Slow Learner

The first time you don't do what OCD wants and your fear drops and **NOTHING BAD HAPPENS**, you're going to feel great. And you should feel great. Teaching OCD to leave you alone is tough. You have taken a big step.

But that first time isn't the only time you're going to need to do it. OCD is a slow learner.

Once you decide on an OCD urge to say no to, you need to resist that urge every time it comes up.

At first, it's best to use the same method each time. Most kids find it's easier that way, because you don't have to figure out what to do each time OCD starts pestering you. When you're ready to pick a different OCD thought or urge to say no to, you can choose a new method. But to begin with, pick one method and stick with it.

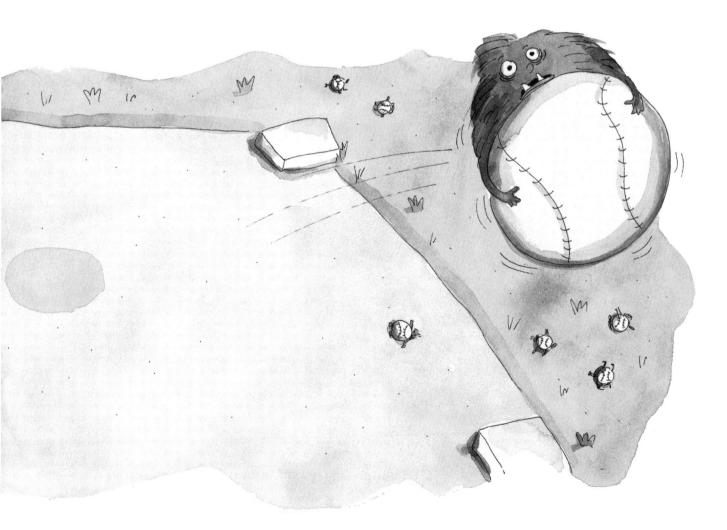

For example, pretend that OCD bothers you about the weather, making you worry that a big storm might be on the way. OCD wants you to check the computer many times a day to see if any storms are coming. Once you decide that you aren't going to listen to OCD about checking the weather, your plan might be to WALK AWAY from OCD.

Draw a child using the walk away method to resist OCD. Be sure to include a speech bubble showing the child talking back to OCD on the way out.

What should the child do after leaving the room?

OCD is a slow learner, but it's clever too.

OCD is clever because it tries to bargain with kids. When OCD realizes that it isn't going to get exactly what it wants, it asks for something slightly different. It's like a child who screams for jelly beans, and when his mom says no, he begs for chocolates instead. Don't be fooled by this.

NO means NO.

Keep Climbing

You know the basics. Now you need to keep climbing, still just one step at a time. Each step is the next OCD message you choose not to obey.

Look back at your list on page 72. Find another OCD thought or urge that you gave a fear rating of 3 or lower, or break one down into smaller parts. Winning against OCD in little ways will help you feel more confident about tackling OCD in bigger ways.

So...

☼ Which OCD urge are you going to stop listening to next?

☼ Which method will you use to show OCD that you are your own boss?

☼ What can you do to keep busy while you're not listening to OCD?

Here are three **DON'TS** to keep in mind while you're fighting OCD:

DON'T STAND AROUND ARGUING WITH OCD

OCD doesn't listen to reason, so you can't convince it that something is safe enough or clean enough or right enough. Talk back once. Then turn your attention to something else, something you would rather be doing.

DON'T LET OCD PULL A SWITCHEROO ON YOU

OCD may try to get you to follow a different ritual, like asking your parents about the weather instead of checking the computer. Or it may try to scream **DANGER!** about something slightly different from before. Remember, this is OCD in disguise. Use your tools against OCD.

Fighting OCD is hard work. Sometimes it might seem too hard. When you can't make it to the step you're working on, take a smaller step. Choose a different urge to fight, or fight just one part of the urge. Practice a step you have already gotten good at.

It's OK to take a break while you're fighting OCD. Hang out for a while on whatever step you're on. When you're climbing a mountain, you don't return to the bottom when you need a rest, you stop where you are. Then, when you're ready, you stand up and take a step. Just one step.

Step by step, you will make it to the top.

Getting Good at Fighting OCD

Some things in life are really hard, but the more you practice, the easier they become.

Think of something you're learning to do, something not related to OCD, that you know will get easier the more you practice. Add it to this scene.

Like any other skill, the more you practice resisting OCD, the easier it becomes. As you get stronger, OCD gets weaker. You begin to see that even though it makes lots of threats, OCD has no power to hurt you.

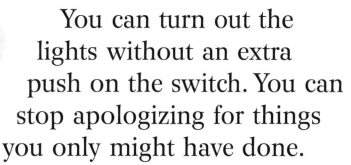

You can turn out the lights without an extra push on the switch. You can stop apologizing for things you only might have done. You can limit your homework time, go to the bathroom just once, and not put on five different shirts trying to find one that feels right. You can throw away the things you are done with, and touch doorknobs, and say goodbye a different way every time.

And **NOTHING BAD WILL HAPPEN.**

Best of all, the nervous feeling that OCD puts into your body will go away all by itself, even though you haven't done what OCD told you to do.

All you need to do is keep using your tools.

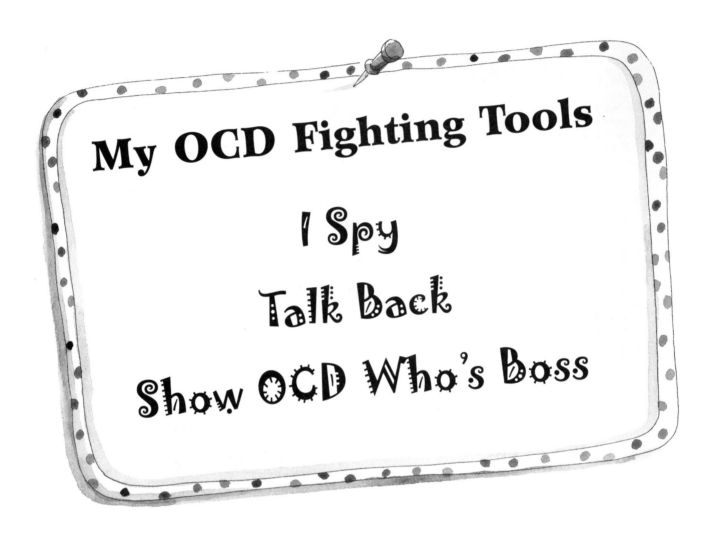

My OCD Fighting Tools

I Spy

Talk Back

Show OCD Who's Boss

Choose one OCD message at a time to say no to. Decide what you're going to do so that OCD is not in charge. Resist OCD's message every time you hear it.

Once you have stopped listening to OCD about that message, choose another OCD message. And another. And another.

Keep track of how well you're doing. Take a jar and fill it with marbles or pennies or anything else that is small. Label the jar OCD. Each time you use a tool to fight OCD, take one of the marbles and put it into a second jar that has your name on it. Watch the OCD jar get emptier while your jar gets fuller.

☼ Draw how you are going to feel as OCD's jar gets emptier and your jar gets fuller.

CHAPTER FOURTEEN

You Can Do It!

You have climbed lots of steps now. You recognize OCD and its bag of tricks. And you have three tools you can use any time OCD is bothering you.

When you use your tools, you are training your brain not to listen to OCD. Your tools are stronger than OCD's tricks.

OCD takes up lots of time. Learning to say no to OCD gives you back your time, so you can do the things you love to do.

Draw yourself doing something you love to do, something you will be able to do more of when OCD isn't such a big part of your life. Be sure to show how happy you will feel.

You can do it! It's going to feel so good.